A **Literature Kit**™ FOR

Cheaper by the Dozen

•••••••••••••••••••

By Frank B. Gilbreth Jr. & Ernestine Gilbreth Carey

Written by Nat Reed

GRADES 7 – 8

Classroom Complete Press

P.O. Box 19729
San Diego, CA 92159
Tel: 1-800-663-3609 | Fax: 1-800-663-3608
Email: service@classroomcompletepress.com

www.classroomcompletepress.com

ISBN-13: 978-1-55319-382-1
ISBN-10: 1-55319-382-2

© 2008

Permission to Reproduce

Critical Thinking Skills

Cheaper by the Dozen

Skills For Critical Thinking	Ch 1-2	Ch 3-4	Ch 5-6	Ch 7-8	Ch 9-10	Ch 11-12	Ch 13-14	Ch 15-16	Ch 17-18	Ch 19	Writing Tasks	Graphic Organizers
LEVEL 1 Knowledge												
• Identify Story Elements	✓	✓	✓	✓	✓	✓	✓	✓	✓	✓	✓	✓
• Recall Details	✓	✓	✓	✓	✓	✓	✓	✓	✓	✓	✓	✓
• Match	✓	✓	✓	✓	✓	✓	✓	✓	✓	✓	✓	✓
• Sequence		✓				✓				✓	✓	
LEVEL 2 Comprehension												
• Compare and Contrast	✓			✓	✓	✓		✓	✓	✓	✓	✓
• Summarize	✓	✓	✓	✓	✓	✓	✓	✓	✓	✓	✓	✓
• State Main Idea		✓							✓	✓	✓	✓
• Describe	✓	✓	✓	✓	✓	✓	✓	✓	✓		✓	✓
• Classify			✓					✓				
LEVEL 3 Application												
• Plan		✓	✓	✓	✓	✓		✓			✓	✓
• Interview					✓		✓			✓		
• Infer Outcomes	✓		✓		✓		✓	✓		✓	✓	✓
LEVEL 4 Analysis												
• Draw Conclusions	✓	✓	✓	✓	✓	✓	✓	✓	✓	✓	✓	✓
• Identify Supporting Evidence			✓					✓	✓	✓	✓	✓
• Infer Character Motivations	✓		✓		✓	✓	✓				✓	✓
• Identify Cause & Effect			✓		✓			✓	✓	✓		✓
LEVEL 5 Synthesis												
• Predict	✓	✓	✓	✓	✓	✓	✓	✓	✓	✓	✓	✓
• Design					✓	✓		✓			✓	✓
• Create		✓	✓		✓	✓					✓	✓
• Write An Alternative Ending To		✓			✓	✓		✓		✓	✓	
LEVEL 6 Evaluation												
• State and Defend An Opinion	✓	✓	✓	✓	✓	✓	✓	✓	✓	✓	✓	✓
• Make Judgements	✓	✓	✓	✓	✓	✓	✓	✓	✓	✓	✓	✓

Based on Bloom's Taxonomy

Contents

✔ **6 BONUS Activity Pages!** Additional worksheets for your students

FREE!

- Go to our website: www.classroomcompletepress.com/**bonus**
- Enter item CC2700 or Cheaper by the Dozen
- Enter pass code CC2700D for Activity Pages

Assessment Rubric

Cheaper by the Dozen

Student's Name: _____ Assignment: _____ Level: _____

	Level 1	Level 2	Level 3	Level 4
Comprehension of Novel • information and details relevant to focus	• Demonstrates a limited understanding of the novel	• Demonstrates a basic understanding of the novel	• Demonstrates a good understanding of the novel	• Demonstrates a thorough understanding of the novel
Content • information and details relevant to focus	• Elements incomplete; key details missing	• Some elements complete; details missing	• All required elements completed; key details contain some description	• All required elements completed; enough description for clarity
Style • effective word choice and originality • precise language	• Little variety in word choice. • Language vague and imprecise	• Some variety in word choice. • Language somewhat vague and imprecise	• Good variety in word choice. • Language precise and quite descriptive	• Writer's voice is apparent throughout. Excellent choice of words. Precise language.
Conventions • spelling, language, capitalization, punctuation	• Errors seriously interfere with the writer's purpose	• Repeated errors in mechanics and usage	• Some errors in convention	• Few errors in convention

STRENGTHS:

WEAKNESSES:

NEXT STEPS:

Teacher Guide

Our resource has been created for ease of use by both
TEACHERS *and* **STUDENTS** *alike.*

Introduction

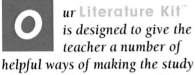

Our **Literature Kit**™ is designed to give the teacher a number of helpful ways of making the study of this novel a more enjoyable and profitable experience for the students. The guide features a number of useful and flexible components, from which the teacher can choose. It is not expected that all of the activities will be completed.

One advantage to this approach to the study of this novel is that the student can work at his/her own speed, and the teacher can assign activities that match the student's abilities.

Our study guide generally divides the novel by chapters and features reading comprehension and vocabulary questions. Themes include coming of age, family/ parental relationships, peer pressure, role models, and the acceptance of responsibilities. *Cheaper by the Dozen* provides a wealth of opportunity for classroom discussion because of its vivid portrayal of family life in the Gilbreth household.

How Is Our Literature Kit™ Organized?

STUDENT HANDOUTS
Chapter Activities *(in the form of reproducible worksheets)* make up the majority of our resource. For each chapter or group of chapters there are BEFORE YOU READ activities and AFTER YOU READ activities.

- The BEFORE YOU READ activities prepare students for reading by setting a purpose for reading. They stimulate background knowledge and experience, and guide students to make connections between what they know and what they will learn. Important concepts and vocabulary from the chapter(s) are also presented.

- The AFTER YOU READ activities check students' comprehension and extend their learning. Students are asked to give thoughtful consideration of the text through creative and evaluative short-answer questions and journal prompts.

Six **Writing Tasks** and three **Graphic Organizers** are included to further develop students' critical thinking and writing skills, and analysis of the text. *(See page 6 for suggestions on using the Graphic Organizers.)* The **Assessment Rubric** *(page 4)* is a useful tool for evaluating students' responses to the Writing Tasks and Graphic Organizers.

PICTURE CUES
Our resource contains three main types of pages, each with a different purpose and use. A **Picture Cue** at the top of each page shows, at a glance, what the page is for.

 Teacher Guide
- Information and tools for the teacher

 Student Handout
- Reproducible worksheets and activities

 Easy Marking™ **Answer Key**
- Answers for student activities

EASY MARKING™ ANSWER KEY
Marking students' worksheets is fast and easy with our **Answer Key**. Answers are listed in columns – just line up the column with its corresponding worksheet, as shown, and see how every question matches up with its answer!

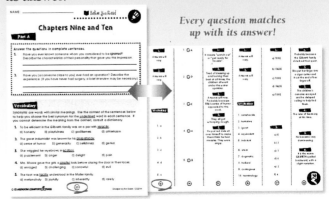

Every question matches up with its answer!

1,2,3
Graphic Organizers

The three **Graphic Organizers** included in our Literature Kit™ are especially suited to a
study of *Cheaper by the Dozen*. Below are suggestions for using each organizer in your classroom,
or they may be adapted to suit the individual needs of your students. The organizers can be used on a projection system or
interactive whiteboard in teacher-led activities, and/or photocopied for use as student worksheets.
To evaluate students' responses to any of the organizers, you may wish to use the **Assessment Rubric** *(on page 4)*.

KWS CHART

The KWS Chart is a useful tool to help students develop
skills in planning and writing a nonfiction article. After having
an initial discussion, ask students to brainstorm topics related to
the novel for further investigation (i.e. early automobiles, sailing,
photography, motion study, tonsils, etc.) Working individually or
in pairs, have students choose one topic from the list to research.
They then jot down what they already know about the topic; what
they would like to know; and possible sources of information.
Have students conduct their research and record information they
found (what they learned). Found on Page 53.

COMPARE / CONTRAST

Cheaper by the Dozen features an array of fascinating
characters, from the opinionated, charismatic Mr. Gilbreth, to his
quiet and gentle wife, Lillian. For this activity the students are to
choose one character from the story to compare/contrast with Mr.
Gilbreth. They are to consider five attributes (physical features and
personality traits) about these two characters and record them in
the left hand column. A variety of attributes should be selected
which are both different and similar, and details should be given
where appropriate. Found on Page 54.

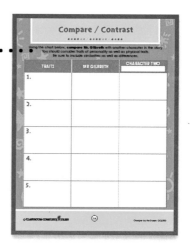

THE FIVE W'S CHART

Students are asked to choose a major event from the novel.
This can be from any section of the book. They are then asked
to complete the accompanying chart with the appropriate
details. This should include, What happened? Who was there?
Why did it happen? When did it happen? Where did it happen?
Found on Page 55.

Bloom's Taxonomy* for Reading Comprehension

The activities in our resource engage and build the full range of thinking skills that are essential for students' reading comprehension. Based on the six levels of thinking in Bloom's Taxonomy, questions are given that challenge students to not only recall what they have read, but move beyond this to understand the text through higher-order thinking. By using higher-order skills of application, analysis, synthesis and evaluation, students become active readers, drawing more meaning from the text, and applying and extending their learning in more sophisticated ways.

Our Literature Kit™, therefore, is an effective tool for any Language Arts program. Whether it is used in whole or in part, or adapted to meet individual student needs, our resource provides teachers with the important questions to ask, inspiring students' interest, creativity, and promoting meaningful learning.

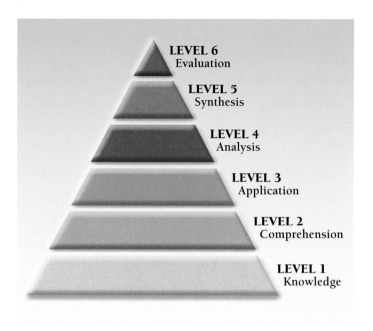

**BLOOM'S TAXONOMY:
6 LEVELS OF THINKING**

Bloom's Taxonomy is a widely used tool by educators for classifying learning objectives, and is based on the work of Benjamin Bloom.

Teaching Strategies — WHOLE-CLASS, SMALL GROUP AND INDEPENDENT STUDY

This study guide contains the following activities:

Before Reading Activities: themes are introduced and thought-provoking questions put forward for the students to consider.

Vocabulary Activities: new and unfamiliar words are introduced and reviewed.

After Reading Questions: the first part of this section includes short answer questions dealing with the content of the play. The second part features questions that are more open-ended and feature concepts from the higher order of Bloom's Taxonomy.

Writing Tasks: creative writing assignments based on Bloom's Taxonomy that relate to the plot of the particular scenes

Graphic Organizers: three full-page reproducible sheets. One has been designed as an alternative to the traditional book report.

Bonus Sheets are also available online.

A **comprehension quiz** is also included comprised of short-answer questions.

The study guide can be used in a variety of ways in the classroom depending on the needs of the students and teacher. The teacher may choose to use an independent reading approach with students capable of working independently. It also works well with small groups, with most of the lessons being quite easy to follow, and finally in other situations, teachers will choose to use it with their entire class.

Teachers may wish to have their students keep a daily reading log so that they might record their daily progress and reflections.

Summary of the Story

Cheaper by the Dozen is the classic story of the Gilbreths, a family with twelve children who grew up in the 1910's and 20's.

Frank and Lillian Gilbreth were renowned efficiency experts, who often practiced their many different theories and experiments on their large family.

Written with wit and humor, the book documents a multitude of humorous and touching vignettes – some hilarious and others nostalgic and heart-warming.

Family adventures include, the family car, a vintage Pierce-Arrow, which is used by the parents for Sunday drives and causes the children no end of embarrassment. A trip out west to visit Mother's straight-laced family. The perilous adventures involving Father's many experiments and notions; getting their tonsils out; skipping grades at school; teaching a lesson to a peeping tom. It is a book with which most families will readily identify, and keep the reader turning the pages to the very end.

Suggestions for Further Reading

SOME NOVELS BY / OR ABOUT THE GILBRETH FAMILY

Belles on their Toes, Frank B. Gilbreth Jr. and Ernestine Gilbreth Carey
Bricklaying System, Frank Gilbreth
Motion Study, Frank Gilbreth
As I Remember, Lillian Gilbreth
Ancestors of the Dozen, Frank B. Gilbreth Jr.
Time Out For Happiness, Frank B. Gilbreth Jr.
Frank and Lillian Gilbreth, Partners For Life, Edna Yost
Jumping Juniper, Ernestine Gilbreth Carey
Giddy Moment, Ernestine Gilbreth Carey

OTHER RECOMMENDED RESOURCES

Little House on the Prairie, © 2007
Number the Stars, © 1998
Bridge to Terabithia, © 1987
All-of-a-kind Family, © 1984
The Dog Who Wouldn't Be, © 1957

Vocabulary

CHAPTERS 1-2

• efficient • elimination • bedlam • composure • converge • incredulous • ominous • intricate • contraption • balk • baritone • inaugurated • extricate • regimentation • gimlet • impressionable • quadrupeds • unrequited • mutilate

CHAPTERS 3-4

• perpetual • contagious • inanimate • sanitary • lurid • vitality • calliope • coincide • subdue • reprobate • pince-nez • leprosy • peril • optimist • fray • penultimate • disposal • dire • elaborate • pompadour

CHAPTERS 5-6

• rendezvous • innuendo • menace • apportion • disreputable • implore • hysterical • atrocious • adept • exotic • prodigy • destiny • rupture • aptitude • apportion • abstain • diplomacy • confident • instinct • duration

CHAPTERS 7-8

• periodic • feted • imposing • regiment • flourish • surreptitiously • acquaintances • ecstasy • militant • prim • acrobatics • sympathetic • introvert • chauffer • courtship • chaperone • inevitable • dignity • patronize • scurvy

CHAPTERS 9-10

• veracity • philanthropy • ecstasy • sinister • tacitly • revel • sedately • reprimand • prevail • salutation • vigor • un-amenable • sarcasm • cornucopia • converge • extricate • infrequent • averred • contagious • consequence

CHAPTERS 11-12

• ramshackle • tentative • igorot • equivalent • indolent • vicinity • recitation • guillotine • lavatory • ominous • stern • albatross • astronomy • accumulate • reluctance • dogmatic • contagious • terminology • invective • derelict

CHAPTERS 13-14

• irritable • blasé • chandelier • conviction • amok • bassinet • comparative • harem • coincide • obstetrically • reconciled • elicit • unanimously • confide • elaborate • resentful • coyly • detest • blanch • fatalistic

CHAPTERS 15-16

• poise • conventional • excruciating • fortitude • demoralize • insolent • devise • lambaste • deceptive • corset • dignity • deputize • deem • anatomy • reprisal • symphony • prominent • implication • stenographer • lambaste

CHAPTERS 17-18

• illicit • detest • emerge • disheveled • indignant • capitulate • innocuous • ukulele • indulge • fatigue • hilt • emancipate • efficient • incredulous • resistance • pneumonia • innocuous • strategic

CHAPTER 19

• principal • subscribe • appraise • fatigue • terrace • intention • symptom • appraising • sophomore • cranium • mumblety-peg • charter • prime • emphasis • stern • alternative • authority • smudge • cremation

Frank B. Gilbreth Jr (1911-2001)
Ernestine Gilbreth Carey (1908-2006)

Frank & Ernestine were two of the twelve children born to Frank (Sr.) and Lillian Gilbreth in the early part of the 20th Century. Married in 1904, Frank Sr. was a pioneer in the field of motion study, and Lillian was a psychologist, earning a doctorate from Brown University.

Although Frank Sr. had no formal education beyond high school, he discovered his vocation when, as a young building contractor, he sought ways to make bricklaying faster and easier. With his wife, he studied the work habits of manufacturing and clerical employees to find methods to increase output and make their jobs easier. He and Lillian eventually founded a management consulting firm called Gilbreth, Inc. Frank Gilbreth Sr. died of heart failure at the relatively young age of 55. His wife, Lillian, survived him by 48 years.

The 12 Gilbreth children were often used as guinea pigs in their father's time-saving experiments. The names of the twelve children were Anne, Mary, **Ernestine**, Martha, **Frank Jr.**, William, Lillian, Fred, Daniel, John, Robert and Jane.

The exploits of the Gilbreth family inspired the book, *Cheaper By the Dozen*, written by two of the Gilbreth children, Frank Jr. and Ernestine. **Frank Jr.** went on to be a journalist, author and newspaper executive in South Carolina. He raised three children of his own. **Ernestine Gilbreth Carey** attended Smith College and graduated with a degree in English. She spent 14 years in buying and management in a New York City department store. Ernestine married and had two children. With her brother, Frank, she was co-recipient of the 1950 French International Humor Award for *Cheaper by the Dozen*.

Did You Know?

- **Mary, was one of the 12 children however she died at a young age, leaving them with only eleven children, they always referred to themselves as a dozen. They simply carried on as if she was still there.**

- **Frank Jr.'s middle initial is B. It stands for Bunker. Named after his father, his full name is Frank Bunker Gilbreth Jr.**

- **Frank was well known for his column, "Doing the Charleston," which he wrote under the pen name Ashley Cooper from the late 1940s to 1993.**

NAME: _____

Chapters One and Two

Part A

Answer the questions in complete sentences.

1. Have you ever played a really funny practical joke on someone? Or perhaps you have been the victim of a practical joke. Tell about a funny practical joke that you were a part of.

_____

_____

2. What do you consider to be three characteristics of a good parent? Explain your choices.

_____

_____

Vocabulary

Choose a word from the list that means the same or nearly the same as the underlined word(s).

> ominous   converge   intricate   composure
> incredulous   inaugurated   elimination   efficient   bedlam

☐	**1.** My brother was most <u>adept</u> at the game of billiards.
☐	**2.** The army general did not rest until he had witnessed the complete <u>eradication</u> of the enemy.
☐	**3.** The arrival of Uncle Buck reduced our home to <u>chaos</u>.
☐	**4.** The racing horse kept his <u>equilibrium</u> even when the other horse's jockey was whipping him.
☐	**5.** All roads seemed to <u>come together</u> at Gettysburg.
☐	**6.** His alibi seemed most <u>suspicious</u>.
☐	**7.** When we spent the night in the old abandoned house, the sudden thunderstorm seemed quite <u>forbidding</u>.
☐	**8.** The treasure map was the most <u>elaborate</u> I have ever seen.
☐	**9.** There was a great ceremony when the battleship was <u>launched</u>.

Chapters One and Two

Part A

1. **Put a check mark (✔) next to the answer that is most correct.**

a) **When the story opens, the Gilbreths lived in:**

○ **A** Baltimore, Maryland
○ **B** Montclair, New Jersey
○ **C** Toronto, Ontario
○ **D** Oakland, California

b) **Mr. Gilbreth worked as:**

○ **A** a diplomat for the federal government
○ **B** an atomic scientist
○ **C** an efficiency expert
○ **D** a coast guard official

c) **By what signal did Mr. Gilbreth gather the family together?**

○ **A** an old fog horn
○ **B** a whistle
○ **C** a bicycle bell
○ **D** by hollering

d) **The Gilbreth's first car was a:**

○ **A** McLaughlin Buick
○ **B** Ford Model T
○ **C** Corvette
○ **D** Pierce Arrow

e) **Which Gilbreth blew the car horn while Mr. Gilbreth was leaning over the engine?**

○ **A** Bill
○ **B** Ernestine
○ **C** Frank Jr.
○ **D** Martha

Chapters One and Two

Part B

Answer the questions in complete sentences or a short paragraph.

1. Describe what the goal of an *efficiency expert* might be:

_____

_____

2. The author says of Mr. Gilbreth, "one reason he had wanted a large family was to assure himself of an appreciative audience…" What does this statement tell you about the personality of this man?

_____

_____

3. Do you agree with this statement from Chapter 1: "He believed that most adults stopped thinking the day they left school." Explain your answer.

_____

_____

4. What were two things that made a car drive for the Gilbreth family something of an adventure.

_____

_____

5. What nickname did Mr. Gilbreth bestow on the family car? Explain why.

_____

_____

Journal Activity

Mr. Gilbreth has many fascinating *idiosyncrasies*. Think of someone you know who is somehow like this character and explain how this person is similar to Mr. Gilbreth, and different.

Chapters Three and Four

Answer the questions in complete sentences.

1. Think of two advantages to growing up in a large family.

   _____

   _____

2. Think of two disadvantages to growing up in a large family.

   _____

   _____

Vocabulary

With a straight line, connect each word on the left with its meaning on the right.

1	perpetual		gruesome	A
2	contagious		disease	B
3	inanimate		vigorous	C
4	sanitary		eyeglasses	D
5	lurid		scoundrel	E
6	vitality		nonliving	F
7	calliope		conquer	G
8	coincide		concur	H
9	subdue		musical instrument	I
10	reprobate		clean	J
11	pince-nez		ceaseless	K
12	leprosy		catching	L

After You Read

Chapters Three and Four

Part A

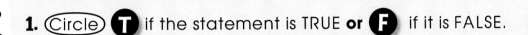

1. (Circle) **T** if the statement is TRUE **or** **F** if it is FALSE.

T F   **a)** Mr. Gilbreth was a skilled driver.

T F   **b)** The family car was kept in a barn.

T F   **c)** Besides getting himself ready for a ride in the car, each older child was responsible for one of the younger ones.

T F   **d)** Mrs. Gilbreth had red hair.

T F   **e)** Bill was the one who first coined the phrase, "cheaper by the dozen".

T F   **f)** Anne objected so strenuously to wearing dusters on their car rides that she swore.

2. Number the events from **1** to **6** in the order they occurred in these chapters.

_____   **a)** While their dad gets the car ready, the kids all get cleaned up and into their dusters.

_____   **b)** Mr. Gilbreth shows off his family to pedestrians.

_____   **c)** Mr. Gilbreth whistles assembly and asks how many want to go for a ride.

_____   **d)** The author recounts Mr. Gilbreth's problem following directions and getting lost.

_____   **e)** Mr. Gilbreth calls roll.

_____   **f)** One of the children who had been especially good was allowed to sit up front.

NAME: _____

Chapters Three and Four

Part B Answer each question with a complete sentence.

1. What do the authors mean when they state that the question was purely *rhetorical* when Mr. Gilbreth asked how many wanted to go for a car ride?

_____

_____

2. Going for a ride in the family car is compared to standing on a roller coaster; volunteering to go onstage for a magician; and doing a back somersault off the high diving board. Think of another activity that might be compared to this.

_____

_____

3. What does Mr. Gilbreth's reluctance to follow simple directions say about his personality?

_____

_____

4. Describe why the ant was one of Mr. Gilbreth's favorite creatures.

_____

_____

5. Why did the Gilbreths not let their children use the washrooms at filling stations?

_____

_____

6. Describe the prank that Bill played on his dad at the end of Chapter 4.

_____

_____

Journal Activity

Describe a road trip that you have taken (by car, train, bus, plane) **or** write about a road trip that you dream one day of taking. What would make this road trip special?

NAME: _____

Chapters Five and Six

| **Part A** | **Answer the questions in complete sentences.** |

1. Mr. Gilbreth is really serious about everything running as efficiently as possible. Can you think of an example in your own life which could do with the help and advice of an **efficiency expert**?

_____

_____

2. Describe one advantage and one disadvantage to having a pet.

_____

_____

Vocabulary — Complete each sentence with a word from the list.

disreputable	implore	adept	innuendo	hysterical
prodigy	apportion	rendezvous	atrocious	menace

1. At the Little Big Horn, General Custer had a _____ with destiny.

2. A subtle _____ never worried Dad.

3. The escaped convict was regarded by all as a _____ to society.

4. My mother will _____ the dessert to all the children equally.

5. The man had a _____ reputation after he was caught stealing from his grandmother.

6. "I _____ you," the woman begged. "Please give me one more chance."

7. Matilda's aunt became _____ when the baby carriage tipped over.

8. The dead fish had an _____ smell.

9. The secretary was most _____ at keyboarding.

10. Clever Ernestine was something of a child _____.

Chapters Five and Six

Part A

1. Fill in each blank with the correct word from the chapters.

a) Grandma Gilbreth prepared her children for their rendezvous with

_____ .

b) When Mr. Gilbreth finished high school, he got a job as a _____ helper.

c) Within a year he had designed a _____ that made him the fastest on the job.

d) Mrs. Gilbreth was from _____ , California and was a

_____ graduate from the University of California.

e) On the employer-employee board, assignments were made on a basis of

personal choice and _____ .

2. Use the words in the box to answer each question.

roller skates	machine	dog	parliamentary	rug

_____

a) At Family Councils, Mr. Gilbreth thought he knew a lot about _____ procedure.

_____

b) At the second meeting of the Family Council, Anne proposed that the family have a voice in the purchase of a _____ .

_____

c) Bill put forth the proposal that the family purchase a _____ .

_____

d) When Lill won the bid for painting the fence, what did her father buy her once the job was done?

_____

e) Mr. Gilbreth insisted on taking Martha to a _____ exhibition in New York.

Chapters Five and Six

Part B

Answer the questions in complete sentences.

1. What do you think is being implied by the statement, "Although a graduate of the University of California, the bride is nonetheless an extremely attractive young woman"?

_____

_____

2. The description in Chapter 5 of the Family Council in operation is quite entertaining. Why do you suppose the parents decided on this format to arrive at the decision about how work would be divided amongst family members?

_____

_____

3. Describe how the children managed to get their parents to agree to the purchase of a family dog.

_____

_____

4. Why did Mr. Gilbreth purchase the Victrolas?

_____

_____

5. What was the reason that Mr. Gilbreth gave for his French being superior to his children's?

_____

_____

Journal Activity

Living in the Gilbreth house would probably be a most interesting experience. Imagine that you are one of the 12 Gilbreth children and write about one of the events described in these two chapters from <u>your</u> point of view.

Chapters Seven and Eight

1. Do you agree with the idea of a student's parent visiting him or her in their classroom now and then? Explain your answer.

_____

_____

Part B

Word List

bedlam
birth
boudoir
boy
car
chat
chauffeur
church
courtship
demeanor
drama
ecstasy
Edsel
Ernestine
fete
genteel
Gilbreth
lurid
many
ominous
periodic
planned
potential
ridiculous
sad
safely
scurvy
seeds
subdue

Across

4. A day of celebration. Holiday.
5. Rapturous delight.
8. The Foolish Carriage was an early one of these.
10. Foreboding.
11. A woman's bedroom.
12. Absurd.
14. Quite a few.
16. Informal conversation.
19. Capable of becoming.
21. Secure from harm.
23. Beginning.
24. Attitude.
25. Noise & confusion.
26. Building of worship.

Down

1. Reoccurring at intervals.
2. A disease.
3. One of the Gilbreth girls.
5. A famous Ford model.
6. To conquer.
7. Unhappy.
9. Dating.
13. Usually the paid driver of a car.
15. Well-bred.
17. Lad.
18. Family name.
19. Schemed.
20. Gruesome.
21. The beginning of plants.
22. Not a comedy.

After You Read

Chapters Seven and Eight

Part A

1. Complete the paragraph by filling in each blank with the correct word from the chapters.

Skipping _____ in school was part of Dad's master plan. The standard
a

reward for skipping was a new_____. Although the Gilbreth children were
b

advanced for their ages in many things, they were only average at best in some

intangibles such as _____ and _____ . According to Mr. Gilbreth,
c   d

his only bad subject was_____. When it came to his children's grades, he was
e

convinced that low marks were merely an error in judgment on the _____ part.
f

At Montclair, the elementary school where four of the younger children attended was

called _____. When describing his children to a teacher, Mr. Gilbreth referred
g

to them as redheads mostly, some blonds, all _____. Although Bill was only
h

supposed to be in grade three, his dad talked the principal into putting him in grade

_____. The children dreaded their dad's surprise visits because he broke all the
i

school _____. Frank Junior's teacher was called Miss _____.
j   k

Mr. Gilbreth went to church only when one of the children was to be _____.
l

He said he believed in God, but couldn't stand _____. He formed this opinion
m

while on his way to _____ on an ocean liner. He did, though, believe in Sunday
n

School, because he thought everyone should have some knowledge of the

_____.
o

Chapters Seven and Eight

Part B

Answer the questions in complete sentences.

1. One of the expressions used to describe Mr. Gilbreth by one of the students is. "your old man is the cat's". How would we express this same thought today?

_____

_____

2. What organization did Mrs. Alice Mebane represent? What was the purpose of this organization?

_____

_____

3. What do you think Mrs. Bruce's real reason was for sending Alice Mebane to interview Mrs. Gilbreth?

_____

_____

4. How was Mr. Gilbreth's final statement in Chapter 7 meant to be funny?

_____

_____

5. How was Mr. Gilbreth able to serve his country during World War I? In your opinion was this an important service? Explain your answer.

_____

_____

6. Why was the visit to Mrs. Gilbreth's family in California such an important event?

_____

Journal Activity

Staying in someone else's home can be hard on a person's nerves. Think of a time when your family either hosted a guest(s), or were hosted yourselves. Describe what it was like for you in this instance. Recall at least one thing you enjoyed, and one thing that was difficult.

NAME: _____

Chapters Nine and Ten

Part A

Answer the questions in complete sentences.

1. Have you ever known someone whom you considered to be **spoiled**? Describe the characteristics of their personality that gave you this impression.

   _____

   _____

2. Have you (or someone close to you) ever had an operation? Describe the experience. (If you have never had surgery, a brief interview may be necessary.)

   _____

   _____

Vocabulary

Synonyms are words with similar meanings. Use the context of the sentences below to help you choose the best synonym for the <u>underlined</u> word in each sentence. If you cannot determine the meaning from the context, consult a dictionary.

1. To be efficient in the Gilbreth family was on a par with **<u>veracity</u>**.
   a) honesty   **b)** playfulness   **c)** godlikeness   **d)** athleticism

2. The great industrialist was known for his **<u>philanthropy</u>**.
   a) sense of humor   **b)** generosity   **c)** selfishness   **d)** genius

3. She wriggled her eyebrows in **<u>ecstasy</u>**.
   a) puzzlement   **b)** anger   **c)** delight   **d)** pain

4. Mrs. Moore gave the girls a **<u>sinister</u>** look before closing the door in their faces.
   a) enraged   **b)** challenging   **c)** sorrowful   **d)** evil

5. The fact was **<u>tacitly</u>** understood in the Moller family.
   a) melancholy   **b)** joyfully   **c)** inherently   **d)** rarely

NAME: _____

Chapters Nine and Ten

Part A

Put a check mark (✔) next to the answer that is most correct.

1. When the Gilbreth children first arrived at their grandparents' home:

- ○ **A**   they regarded their mother's parents with awe
- ○ **B**   their throats were extremely irritated by the smog
- ○ **C**   Anne immediately became homesick and had to be sent home
- ○ **D**   the family cat went missing

2. Billy's rebellion was caused by:

- ○ **A**   a letter from his dad
- ○ **B**   him being forced to cut the grass
- ○ **C**   a kiss from his aunt
- ○ **D**   a pair of pants

3. Three places where the children were taken to visit were:

- ○ **A**   Mexico, the movies, the Grand Canyon
- ○ **B**   Chinatown, Los Angeles, Edinburgh
- ○ **C**   the movies, San Francisco, Inverness
- ○ **D**   Phoenix, San Francisco, Salt Lake City

4. What surgery did Dr. Burton feel it was essential that many of the Gilbreth children undergo?

- ○ **A**   tonsils
- ○ **B**   appendix
- ○ **C**   hangnail
- ○ **D**   wisdom teeth

5. Which daughter was operated on "by mistake"?

- ○ **A**   Martha
- ○ **B**   Ernestine
- ○ **C**   Anne
- ○ **D**   Lillian

Chapters Nine and Ten

Part B

Answer the questions in complete sentences.

1. <u>Investigate</u>: Mrs. Gilbreth says in Chapter 9, "… when they decide to feel at home they may decide all at once. If they do, it's **Katey bar the door**." Find out what this unusual expression means. (Hint: the internet might be a help.)

_____

_____

2. Describe the circumstance leading to the children getting soaking wet in Chapter 9.

_____

_____

3. Why do you think the cook got along so well with Billy?

_____

_____

4. What made the train trip home from California so uncomfortable?

_____

_____

5. Describe the practical joke that Mr. Gilbreth played on his wife and mother, and describe the reaction to his joke.

_____

_____

Journal Activity

The Gilbreth are renowned motion experts. Each day you perform a multitude of actions in your school classroom. Some of these actions probably entail motions that the Gilbreth's would consider wasteful. In your journal rethink one of the common actions you perform on a daily basis (i.e. getting your pencil sharpened, handing in an assignment to the teacher, delivering the attendance to the office). Now design and describe a way of performing this action so that it is more efficient than the way it is presently done.

Chapters Eleven and Twelve

Part A   Answer the questions in complete sentences.

1. In Chapter 11 the Gilbreth family go on vacation. What is the most memorable vacation you have ever taken – or tell about a vacation that you would like to take.

_____

_____

2. The Gilbreth family try their hand at sailing in Chapter 12. What do you think would be an advantage to sailing over operating a motorized boat? What might be a disadvantage? Which would you prefer? Explain your answer.

_____

_____

Vocabulary   Choose a word from the list to complete each definition.

terminology	indolent	stern	dogmatic	contagious
equivalent	halliard	ramshackle	tentative	igorot

1. The Heffernins lived in a _____ cottage.

2. Sarah took a _____ step into the abandoned house.

3. The _____ people live in the mountains of the Philippines.

4. Ten dollars back then is the _____ of almost a hundred dollars today.

5. My mother's new secretary is so _____, I doubt if she will last the week.

6. The boat's outboard motor is usually on the _____ of the craft.

7. As captain of the vessel, Mr. Gilbreth's orders were most _____ in nature.

8. The _____, which was connected to the sail, broke in the storm.

9. The sailor's enthusiasm was _____ among the crew.

10. When I joined the navy I had to learn a lot of new _____.

 Before You Read

Chapters Eleven and Twelve

Part A

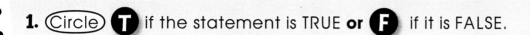

1. (Circle) **T** if the statement is TRUE **or** **F** if it is FALSE.

T F **a)** The Gilbreth family spent their summers at Nantucket, Massachusetts.

T F **b)** Mr. Gilbreth named the cottage *The Lighthouse*.

T F **c)** A **Therblig** is a *unit of motion* or *thought*.

T F **d)** The Gilbreth's catboat was called the **Catamaran**.

T F **e)** Mr. Gilbreth was struck on the head by the boom and was knocked overboard.

2. Number the events from **1** to **6** in the order they occurred in the chapters.

_____ **a)** Tom Grieves admits to showing tourists through the cottage when the Gilbreths were not at home.

_____ **b)** Two canaries escape while on route to the cottage.

_____ **c)** Mr. Gilbreth purchases two lighthouses and a ramshackle cottage.

_____ **d)** A catboat is purchased.

_____ **e)** The Gilbreths spend a night in a hotel in New London, Connecticut.

_____ **f)** The Gilbreth children learn Morse code.

NAME: _____

Chapters Eleven and Twelve

Part B · **Answer each question with a complete sentence.**

1. Speculate as to why the Whitneys moved their cottage a mile away.

_____

_____

2. Describe how Ernestine lost the top of her finger.

_____

_____

3. Describe the circumstances that caused the captain of the steamer to delay their trip to the island. How was the incident finally resolved?

_____

_____

4. <u>Investigate</u>: at one point in Chapter 11, Mr. Gilbreth says, "Last one in is Kaiser Bill." Historically, who was **Kaiser Bill**.

_____

_____

5. Describe how Mr. Gilbreth's personality changed once aboard the family boat.

_____

_____

6. How did Mr. Gilbreth come by the name Therblig?

_____

_____

Journal Activity

Imagine that you have been granted the holiday of your dreams. What would it entail? Would you wish for a summer at a cottage like the Gilbreths'? Or would you rather spend a couple of weeks on a desert island in the South Pacific? Write a journal entry describing in detail your dream vacation. Be sure to document not only the location, but also the events you would plan in order to make it a most memorable holiday.

📖 *Before You Read*

Chapters Thirteen and Fourteen

Part A **Answer the questions in complete sentences.**

1. Getting a new member of the family can be an exciting event. Describe one benefit this new member might bring to the family.

   _____

   _____

2. Learning the origin of family names is often fascinating. Investigate the meaning and/or origin of your first name and surname.

   _____

   _____

Vocabulary

Circle **the correct word(s) that matches the meaning of the underlined word.**

1. Mr. Gilbreth was very underlined:irritable after his unexpected dunking in the ocean.

   a) drenched   **b)** cranky   **c)** terrified   **d)** solemn

2. Dad was reconciled to his fate.

   a) resigned   **b)** furious   **c)** expensive   **d)** diligent

3. I thought it wise to confide in someone before my date in court.

   a) scarce   **b)** take   **c)** turn   **d)** discuss privately

4. There was no elaborate praise for the little monkey.

   a) selfish   **b)** uncomplicated   **c)** extravagant   **d)** frightening

5. The professor was most resentful when his class was interrupted.

   a) annoyed   **b)** pleased   **c)** self-absorbed   **d)** confused

6. Mrs. Gilbreth acted coyly when interviewed.

   a) most offended   **b)** bravely   **c)** ignorantly   **d)** bashfully

Chapters Thirteen and Fourteen

Part A

1. **Fill in each blank with the correct word from the chapters.**

a) Mr. And Mrs. Gilbreth were married in _____, California.

b) When Mrs. Gilbreth was expecting their first child, her husband confided in her that he believed all their children would be _____.

c) Their first child was called _____.

d) Mr. Gilbreth wanted the nurse to speak _____ in front of the baby.

e) Shortly after the family moved to Plainfield, New Jersey, _____ was born.

2. **Use the words in the box to answer each question.**

| William | Lillian | Robert | Frank | Jane |

a) Mr. Gilbreth wanted to name the fifth child _____.

b) Instead they named the child _____.

c) The sixth child, born in Providence, was named _____.

d) Which child was the youngest of the Gilbreths?

e) Which son was named after no one in particular, but only because his mother liked the name?

Chapters Thirteen and Fourteen

Part B **Answer each question with a complete sentence.**

1. When Mrs. Gilbreth attempted to explain the facts of life to her children, what two things did they learn more about?

_____

_____

2. When Jane was born what was Mrs. Gilbreth's impression of having a baby in the hospital?

_____

_____

3. **a)** Why did Mr. Gilbreth like to take photographs instead of hiring a photographer?

_____

_____

b) What was there about his picture-taking that proved to be a terrifying experience for his younger children?

_____

_____

c) What sometimes happened when he took a picture of the family using a delayed-action release?

_____

_____

Journal Activity

Not many families get to welcome as many new members as did the Gilbreths. Describe from your own experience (or imagination) the arrival of a new member into your family. Describe your own personal feelings involving this experience and the circumstances themselves. You may wish to interview a friend and record their experiences in your journal.

Chapters Fifteen and Sixteen

Part A   **Answer the questions in complete sentences.**

1. Babysitting can be a difficult, thankless job. If possible, draw upon your own experiences as a babysitter, or perhaps when you were *babysat*, and describe two things about this responsibility that would not be easy.

_____

_____

2. In Chapter 15 a visiting psychologist subjected the Gilbreth children to a number of tests. Many people find taking tests to be a nerve-wracking experience. Do you think that tests are the best way for teachers to find out what a student knows about something, or can you think of an alternative way that this data might be gathered?

_____

_____

Vocabulary   **Write a sentence using the following words. Make sure that the meaning of each word is clear in your sentence.**

a) poise _____

b) conventional _____

c) excruciating _____

d) fortitude _____

e) demoralize _____

f) insolent _____

g) devise _____

h) lambaste _____

i) deceptive _____

Chapters Fifteen and Sixteen

Part A

1. **Complete the paragraph by filling in each blank with the correct word from the chapters.**

Mrs. Gilbreth often objected to her husband's methods of discipline, telling him, "Not on the end of the _____." Skull-_____ and elbow- _____
      a   **b**   **c**
became a common disciplinary practice. George Isles, a Canadian author, took a special liking to _____. One day when their guest, Russell Allen, belched
                           d
at the supper table, Jack told him that he was in no mood for an _____
                                                  e
recital. After Jack apologized to Mr. Allen, Mr. Gilbreth admitted that it was really his fault. The children's aunt _____ lived a few blocks from them. She was very
                            f
accomplished at playing the _____, so Mr. Gilbreth decided it would be a
                               g
good idea for his children to take lessons from her. Although her nieces and nephews had no musical talent, she gave them lessons for _____ years. The Gilbreth
                                       h
children were allowed to play at the annual _____. Like Grandma, their aunt
                                        i
thought all _____ were shiftless.
             j

2. **Put a check mark (✔) next to the most appropriate answer:**

a) The psychologist asked, "Does it hurt:

- ○ **A** when your mother spanks you?
- ○ **B** to be alone all the time?
- ○ **C** to have such large feet?
- ○ **D** to skip so many grades?

b) Which Gilbreth cooked up the plot against the psychologist?:

- ○ **A** Lillian
- ○ **B** Bill
- ○ **C** Anne
- ○ **D** Ernestine

c) On Friday nights Dad and Mom:

- ○ **A** studied German together
- ○ **B** went to bed early
- ○ **C** went to the movies
- ○ **D** worked on a book together

d) Dad's favorite movie was:

- ○ **A** The Grapes of Wrath
- ○ **B** Over the Hill to the Poor House
- ○ **C** The Magnificent Seven
- ○ **D** The Great Escape

Chapters Fifteen and Sixteen

Part A   Answer each question with a complete sentence.

1. Using a source such as *Wikipedia*, check out what **Esperanto** is all about.

_____

_____

2. What is your impression of Mr. Gilbreth's disciplinary methods with his children? Did they appear to be effective? Defend your answer.

_____

_____

3. Describe the kind of babysitter that Aunt Anne was.

_____

_____

4. Describe one of the skits that the Gilbreth children performed for their parents.

_____

_____

5. Why do you think the use of exaggeration was so effective in the children's skits?

_____

_____

6. Reread the Messrs. Jones and Bones skit in Chapter 16. This passage has been called *blatantly racist, and completely unacceptable in today's society.* Do you agree with this statement? Defend your answer.

_____

_____

Journal Activity   **Imagine that you were an African American boy or girl and overheard the Messrs. Jones and Bones skit. Record in your journal how this skit made you feel.**

NAME: _____

Chapters Seventeen and Eighteen

Part B   Answer the questions in complete sentences.

1. **Styles** certainly do change from generation to generation (and sometimes even from year to year). Think of an example of how styles have changed since your parents were your age (i.e. clothing or hair styles).

_____

_____

2. In Chapter 17 the older Gilbreth girls find some of their father's rules quite hard to take. Do you think that children should have some input into the rules established by their parents? Explain your answer.

_____

_____

Vocabulary   In each of the following sets of words, underline the one word which does not belong. Then write a sentence explaining why it does not fit.

1. illicit	illegal	contagious	prohibited
2. detest	despise	hate	resist
3. descend	emerge	arise	arrive
4. disheveled	plush	sloppy	rumpled
5. indignant	annoyed	irritated	agreeable
6. courtly	capitulate	surrender	concede
7. innocuous	bland	intent	banal

Chapters Seventeen and Eighteen

Part A

Put a check mark (✔) next to the answer that is most correct.

1. **Mr. Gilbreth threatened the girls with sending them to a:**

- ○ **A** private school
- ○ **B** school for girls
- ○ **C** convent
- ○ **D** military academy

2. **Mr. Gilbreth claimed that this was the only thing the girls were interested in.**

- ○ **A** being popular
- ○ **B** boys
- ○ **C** their grades
- ○ **D** fast cars

3. **After giving in on the *hair* question, the girls began to work on him regarding changes in:**

- ○ **A** shoes
- ○ **B** makeup
- ○ **C** going to parties
- ○ **D** dress

4. **When Mr. Gilbreth wasn't able to chaperone one of his daughter's on their dates, whom did he send?**

- ○ **A** Mrs. Gilbreth
- ○ **B** Frank or Bill
- ○ **C** Aunt Anne
- ○ **D** Tom Grieves

5. **Mr. Gilbreth referred to his wife as:**

- ○ **A** Captain, My Captain
- ○ **B** Darling Dearie
- ○ **C** Boss
- ○ **D** all of the above

NAME: _____

Chapters Seventeen and Eighteen

Part B **Answer each question with a complete sentence.**

1. Chapter 17 features a number of terms peculiar to the 1920's. Investigate and define <u>one</u> of the following terms (as it pertained to this era): *flapper, sheik, galoshes, slickers, chic, shifters club or cootie garages.*

_____

_____

2. In her relationship with her father, why did Anne feel a certain amount of responsibility toward her younger sisters?

_____

_____

3. What drastic measures did Anne take in Chapter 17 that upset her mother so much? Why did she take this action?

_____

_____

4. Why didn't the girls want their mother to have her hair bobbed?

_____

_____

5. What did Anne mean when she described her father as *the belle of the high-school ball*? What was the implication for Anne and her sisters?

_____

_____

6. Describe the lesson the Gilbreths taught Motorcycle Mac.

_____

Journal Activity **Imagine that you were Motorcycle Mac. Write a journal entry explaining your side of the story.**

© CLASSROOM COMPLETE PRESS **37** **Cheaper by the Dozen CC2700**

NAME: _____

Chapter Nineteen

Part A   **Answer the questions in complete sentences.**

1. The loss of a close family member can be a most traumatic event. Either from your own personal experience, or your imagination, describe what it must be like for a family to lose a loved-one. You may wish to interview someone you know who has suffered such a loss in order to record their feelings in this matter.

_____

_____

2. Compare Mr. Gilbreth to a dad that you know. How are they similar? How are they different?

_____

_____

Vocabulary   **Choose a word from the list that means the same as the underlined word.**

charter	fatigue	cranium	terrace
principal	subscribe	appraise	prime

☐	**1.** The responsibilities of his job seem to be the <u>main</u> reason for him being away so often.
☐	**2.** Do you <u>consent</u> to the idea that a St. Bernard is the bravest of all dogs?
☐	**3.** She was hired to <u>assess</u> the worth of the painting.
☐	**4.** The marathon runner collapsed from <u>exhaustion</u>.
☐	**5.** Jackie was sitting on the <u>veranda</u>.
☐	**6.** Mother is going to <u>lease</u> a boat for the summer.
☐	**7.** His <u>skull</u> was covered with little bumps.
☐	**8.** Mr. Gilbreth thought he was in the <u>zenith</u> of his life.

Chapter Nineteen

Part A

1. (Circle) **T** if the statement is TRUE **or** **F** if it is FALSE.

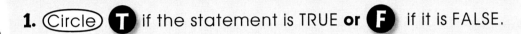

     T   F   **a)** Mr. Gilbreth had been suffering from a bad heart for years.

     T   F   **b)** Mr. Gilbreth was only sixty-five years old when evidence of his poor health began to been seen by the children.

     T   F   **c)** His poor health was known to Mrs. Gilbreth even before their oldest child was born.

     T   F   **d)** Mr. Gilbreth made arrangements to have his heart donated to Princeton University.

     T   F   **e)** Anne, the oldest Gilbreth daughter, broke the news of their father's death to the rest of the children.

     T   F   **f)** At Mr. Gilbreth's funeral he was dressed in his army uniform.

2. Number the events from **1** to **6** in the order they occurred in these chapters.

_____ **a)** Mr. Gilbreth dies suddenly.

_____ **b)** Mr. Gilbreth's ashes were scattered into the Atlantic Ocean.

_____ **c)** Mrs. Gilbreth decides to go to London and Prague to fulfill her husband's speaking engagements.

_____ **d)** Mr. Gilbreth begins losing weight, and is told he is dying.

_____ **e)** Mr. Gilbreth makes arrangements to be an organ donor.

_____ **f)** Mr. Gilbreth informs his doctor that he intends to outlive the physician and attend his funeral.

Chapter Nineteen

Part B   **Answer each question with a complete sentence.**

1. In what two ways did Mr. Gilbreth's deteriorating health manifest itself?

_____

_____

2. What was the maximum amount of time that Dr. Burton gave Mr. Gilbreth to live?

_____

_____

3. Why do you think Mr. Gilbreth decided to be an organ donor?

_____

_____

4. What world event caused motion study to be emphasized more and more?

_____

_____

5. How did Mrs. Gilbreth change after her husband's death? Why do you think this happened?

_____

_____

6. What sacrifices were necessary for the family to make after their father's death?

_____

_____

Journal Activity

The death of a loved one can be a life-altering experience. Imagine you are one of the Gilbreth children. Write a journal entry expressing your innermost feelings following the death of your father.

Chapters 1 to 3

F. W. Taylor

Frederick Winslow Taylor (1856 – 1915) and his work on **Time Study**, is credited with assisting the Gilbreths in their pioneering work on Motion Study. Taylor, a mechanical engineer, was primarily interested in improving industrial efficiency in the late 19th Century. This was very important to industries at this time in world history.

> **Investigate the life and achievements of F.W. Taylor, and prepare a short report of about a page in length documenting this man's life and principal achievements. Be sure to include his accomplishments, and also why he devoted his life to this work.**

Chapters 4 to 6

An Acrostic Poem

An Acrostic poem is one in which the first letters of each line are aligned vertically to form a word. The word often is the subject of the poem.

>
> *Don't 12 kids*
> *Often seem like a*
> *Zillion?*
> *Especially*
> *Near bedtime?*

Make up your own Acrostic Poem. Use for your subject a theme from the book (i.e. Gilbreth, carriage, astronomy, motion, photo, twelve).

Chapters 7 to 9

This activity is especially for students with an artistic flair or who love comic books! It can be done for any of incidents described so far in **Cheaper by the Dozen**.

> The first step is to decide on the length of your comic strip (6 to 12 frames is suggested); next consider what events you will include. You may wish to highlight a brief incident (i.e. going for a ride in the Foolish Carriage), or encompass the highlights of a chapter – or even the first nine chapters. You may even want to provide an alternate ending to your scene!

A quick sketch of the comic strip can first be accomplished in a **storyboard format** before a final, good copy is attempted. The strip should include a title, dialog, and color. It should be neat and imaginative.

- -

Chapters 10 to 12

Express Your Opinion

At the turn of the last century, many people greeted the advent of the automobile with fear and hostility. Like a lot of major changes, people were very leery about this strange new invention, and they warned about the dire consequences of such a device taking over for the horse. In fact for a time the automobile was known as the "horseless carriage".

Imagine you are the editor of a small newspaper in Nantucket during the time when the Gilbreths and their *Foolish Carriage* could be seen on the area's roads. You have decided to write an editorial expressing your concerns about the automobile taking over for the horse and carriage. Write this editorial for your newspaper expressing your concerns regarding the matter, supporting your position with facts and reason. The purpose of your editorial is to convince your readers of the dangers of this invention, and the frightening consequences which could result from its taking over the nation's highways. The editorial should be approximately one-half page in length.

Chapters 13 to 16

Dear Only Child

Imagine you are one of the Gilbreth children. **Write a letter** to a friend or relative who is an only child and lives in another city. It would probably be very difficult for this person to even imagine what it would be like to live in such a large family, so be sure to describe some of the hardships that come from living in a family with eleven brothers and sisters. Please be sure to include specific examples (from the book or your imagination) of some of the challenges that come with sharing the house with so many people.

Your perspective may be influenced by where you rank in birth order in the family (i.e. whether you are the oldest, youngest, or somewhere in between). You may wish to balance the letter somewhat by describing one or two things that are really great about living in such a large family. Happy writing!

- -

Chapters 17 to 19

By this point in the novel we have met all of the major characters of **Cheaper by the Dozen**. Imagine now that you are a casting director of a major motion picture studio who is about to make another feature length film of this book.

> **Your task is to cast each of the following characters using only people (students, teachers, etc.) from your school. For each character, write down who you have chosen to play the role and briefly explain why you selected that individual.**
>
> - Frank Gilbreth Sr.
> - Frank Gilbreth Jr.
> - Dr. Burton
> - Aunt Anne
> - Lillian Gilbreth (the mother)
> - Billy Gilbreth
> - Motorcycle Mac

Word Search

Find the following key words from the story. The words are written horizontally, vertically, diagonally and some are even backwards.

chaperone	destiny	implore	philosophical
chic	detest	instinct	revel
conceited	ecstasy	leeward	sarcasm
coyly	feted	lurid	sinister
debutante	Gilbreth	mooring	waive

y	x	v	m	r	e	v	e	l	u	q	g	a	b	i	f
n	p	h	i	l	o	s	o	p	h	i	c	a	l	m	e
i	f	h	n	n	d	i	r	u	l	m	i	e	r	p	t
t	g	a	t	k	r	a	f	b	h	s	w	a	i	v	e
s	i	n	i	s	t	e	r	e	i	g	d	a	z	e	d
e	j	h	i	f	d	e	t	i	e	c	n	o	c	s	t
d	c	a	v	f	t	h	f	n	o	k	e	e	h	s	y
l	s	s	w	h	i	o	e	s	t	u	t	r	a	e	l
o	e	a	t	d	e	b	u	t	a	n	t	e	p	d	y
u	o	e	a	a	j	a	b	i	p	v	i	c	e	o	o
s	i	d	w	t	s	i	u	n	s	o	c	c	r	r	c
l	r	d	s	a	e	y	f	c	g	n	i	r	o	o	m
c	h	i	c	s	r	l	u	t	e	l	y	c	n	b	s
a	s	e	l	d	o	d	e	t	e	s	t	i	e	s	i
i	m	p	l	o	r	e	t	e	m	s	a	c	r	a	s

Cheaper by the Dozen CC2700

Comprehension Quiz

Answer each question in a complete sentence.

1. What nickname did they give to the family car?

_____

_____

2. In what subject did Mrs. Gilbreth receive her university training?

_____

_____

3. Which of the Gilbreth boys was known as a practical joker?

_____

_____

4. When would Mr. Gilbreth typically use the comment, "*Not of general interest*"?

_____

_____

5. How was Mr. Gilbreth typically received by the teachers of his children when he paid a surprise visit?

_____

_____

6. To what city in California did Mrs. Gilbreth take her children to visit her family?

_____

_____

7. What surgical procedure did Dr. Burton perform on a number of the Gilbreths (including the father)?

_____

_____

SUBTOTAL: /14

Comprehension Quiz

8.   Describe the effect that the surgery had on Mr. Gilbreth.

_____

_____

(2)

9.   Describe the unusual technique that Mr. Gilbreth used to help his children
learn Morse Code.

_____

_____

(2)

10.   What was the Rena and how did the Rena amuse the children during the
summer?

_____

_____

(2)

11.   What had Motorcycle Mac done that upset the Gilbreth children so much?

_____

_____

(2)

12.   Describe how Mr. Gilbreth upset his daughters' dates.

_____

_____

(2)

13.   How many daughters did the Gilbreth family have before their first son,
Frank Jr., was born?

_____

_____

(2)

14.   What caused Mr. Gilbreth's death?

_____

_____

(2)

SUBTOTAL: /14

Cheaper by the Dozen CC2700

(11)

1. Answers will vary

2. Answers will vary

Vocabulary

1. efficient
2. elimination
3. bedlam
4. composure
5. converge
6. incredulous
7. ominous
8. intricate
9. inaugurated

(12)

1.
a) **B**
b) **C**
c) **B**
d) **D**
e) **A**

(13)

1. Answers will vary, i.e. an expert at helping companies save money by becoming more cost-efficient and doing things faster and less expensively.

2. He liked to be the center of attention.

3. Answers will vary.

4. The car was temperamental and Mr. Gilbreth liked to draw attention to his large family.

5. The Foolish Carriage.

(14)

1. Answers will vary

2. Answers will vary

Vocabulary

1	K
2	L
3	F
4	J
5	A
6	C
7	I
8	H
9	G
10	E
11	D
12	B

(15)

1.
a) **FALSE**
b) **TRUE**
c) **TRUE**
d) **TRUE**
e) **FALSE**
f) **TRUE**

2.
a) **2**
b) **5**
c) **1**
d) **6**
e) **3**
f) **4**

(16)

1. He didn't really expect an answer.

2. Answers will vary.

3. Answers will vary, i.e. He has a lot of self-confidence.

4. It was very industrious / didn't waste anything / showed teamwork.

5. They thought them to be dirty.

6. He pretended to be his mother and would tell his father to drive more slowly.

EZ✔

EZ✓

1. Answers will vary. i.e. Your dad's alright.

2. Some sort of national birth control organization.

3. For a little fun.

4. Answers will vary. This was something Mrs. Mebane was fond of saying to Mrs. Gilbreth.

5. He was assigned to motion study training in assembling and disassembling weapons. Answers will vary.

6. She hadn't been home for years, and her children hadn't met her family yet.

(22)

1.

a) grades

b) bicycle

c) leadership
d) sociability
e) spelling
f) teacher's

g) Nishuane

h) speckled

i) five
j) rules
k) Billsop
l) christened
m) clergymen
n) Europe

o) Bible

(21)

---

1. Answers will vary.

Across
4. fete
5. ecstasy
8. car
10. ominous
11. boudoir
12. ridiculous
14. many
16. chat
19. potential
21. safely
23. birth
24. demeanor
25. bedlam
26. church

Down
1. periodic
2. scurvy
3. Ernestine
5. Edsel
6. subdue
7. sad
9. courtship
13. chauffeur
15. genteel
17. boy
18. Gilbreth
19. planned
20. lurid
21. seeds
22. drama

(20)

---

1. Most women university graduates are unattractive.

2. Answers will vary. Perhaps to help the children feel an ownership on the allotment of responsibilities.

3. They passed a motion to buy a less expensive rug, and then used the savings to purchase a dog.

4. So the children could learn to speak French by listening to the records.

5. He learned the language in Paris.

(19)

1.

a) destiny

b) bricklayer's

c) scaffold

d) Oakland, psychology

e) aptitude

2.

a) parliamentary

b) rug

c) dog

d) roller skates

e) machine

(18)

---

1. Answers will vary.

2. Answers will vary.

Vocabulary

1. rendezvous

2. innuendo

3. menace

4. apportion

5. disreputable

6. implore

7. hysterical

8. atrocious

9. adept

10. prodigy

(17)

1. Answers will vary.

2. Answers will vary.

Vocabulary

1. a
2. b
3. c
4. d
5. c

(23)

1. A
2. D
3. C
4. A
5. B

(24)

1. It means "watch out" or "get ready for trouble".

2. Tired of dressing up and looking their best at all times, the children all went under the water sprinkler.

3. Answers will vary. Probably because Billy's sense of humor appealed to the cook.

4. They all got whooping cough.

5. He put red dots all over himself to make them think he had measles. They were angry.

(25)

1. Answers will vary.

2. Answers will vary.

Vocabulary

1. ramshackle
2. tentative
3. igorot
4. equivalent
5. indolent
6. stern
7. dogmatic
8. halliard
9. contagious
10. terminology

(26)

1.
a) TRUE
b) FALSE
c) TRUE
d) FALSE
e) TRUE

2.
a) 5
b) 3
c) 1
d) 6
e) 2
f) 4

(27)

1. Probably because the Gilbreth family disturbed their quiet.

2. She put her finger into a cigar cutter and it cut the end of her finger off.

3. The children's canaries escaped and he delayed sailing to help find them.

4. The ruler of Germany at this time.

5. He became very domineering.

6. It is the name GILBRETH spelled backward, with a slight variation.

(28)

EZ✓

1. It is an international auxiliary language.

2. Answers will vary.

3. Although stern, she had some difficulty controlling the children.

4. Answers will vary. The skits usually poked fun at family members, especially the parents.

5. Answers will vary.

6. Answers will vary.

34

1.
a) spine
b) rapping
c) thumping
d) Lillian
e) organ
f) Anne
g) piano
h) six
i) recitals
j) Irishmen

2.
a) ⊘ A   b) ⊘ D
c) ⊘ C   d) ⊘ B

33

---

1. Answers will vary

2. Answers will vary

Vocabulary
Answers will vary

32

---

1. Botany and apiology.

2. She thought it was marvelous.

3a. He thought he was better than a professional photographer.

3b. The flash.

3c. He would get a picture of himself moving into the scene, or taking a swing at one of the children.

31

1.
a) Oakland
b) girls
c) Anne
d) German
e) Martha

2.
a) Lillian
b) Frank
c) William
d) Jane
e) Robert

30

---

1. Answers will vary

2. Answers will vary

Vocabulary
1. b
2. a
3. d
4. c
5. a
6. d

29

1. Answers will vary.

2. Answers will vary.

Vocabulary

Reasons will vary.

1. contagious
2. resist
3. descend
4. plush
5. agreeable
6. courtly
7. intent

(35)

---

1. C

2. A

3. D

4. B

5. D

(36)

---

1. Answers will vary.

2. She was the oldest.

3. She cut her hair. Rebellion – it was more efficient to care for.

4. They wanted her to look like a mother, not a silly flapper.

5. He was the center of attention – not them.

6. When they found him peeping in the girls' bedroom window, they pretended they were going to burn down the tree he was in.

(37)

---

1. Answers will vary

2. Answers will vary

Vocabulary

1. principal
2. subscribe
3. appraise
4. fatigue
5. terrace
6. charter
7. cranium
8. prime

(38)

1.
a) TRUE
b) FALSE
c) FALSE
d) FALSE
e) FALSE
f) TRUE

2.
a) 4
b) 5
c) 6
d) 1
e) 3
f) 2

(39)

---

1. Two of: He lost weight; his hands trembled; his face was gray; he didn't have as much energy.

2. A year.

3. Answers will vary. Perhaps because he thought his brain to be extra-ordinary.

4. Postwar industrial expansion.

5. She became more dominant. Answers will vary.

6. They let the cook go; sold the car; and live very simply.

EZ✓

(40)

Word Search Answers

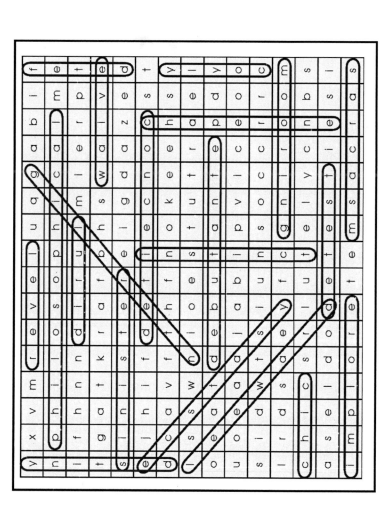

8. He did not handle the procedure well, he complained a lot and took a long time to recover.

9. He would leave messages written in Morse Code laying around the house for the children to solve.

10. A sailing boat in which their father taught them to sail.

11. He tried to peek through the girls' bedroom window.

12. He went with them as a chaperone.

13. Four.

14. A heart attack.

1. Foolish Carriage.

2. Psychology.

3. Bill.

4. When a topic of conversation at the dinner table made him uncomfortable.

5. They were happy to see him.

6. Oakland.

7. The removal of their tonsils.

46

45

44

KWS Chart

· · · · · · · · · · · · · · · · · · · ·

Choose a topic or theme addressed in **Cheaper by the Dozen** (i.e. early automobiles, sailing, photography, motion study, tonsils). Add details to each column making it possible for a researcher to write a report on the topic.

Topic:

What I Know:	What I Want to Learn:	Possible Sources:

Compare / Contrast

Using the chart below, **compare Mr. Gilbreth** with another character in the story. You should consider traits of personality as well as physical traits. Be sure to include similarities as well as differences.

TRAITS	MR GILBRETH	CHARACTER TWO
1.		
2.		
3.		
4.		
5.		

The Five W's Chart

Choose a **major event** from the novel, then complete the following chart with the appropriate details.

What happened?

_____

_____

Who was there?

_____

_____

Why did it happen?

_____

_____

When did it happen?

_____

_____

Where did it happen?

_____

_____